30
PLANES
FOR THE
PAPER PILOT

30
PLANES
FOR THE
PAPER PILOT

Peter Vollheim

ILLUSTRATED WITH LINE DRAWINGS AND
PHOTOGRAPHS

PUBLISHED BY POCKET BOOKS NEW YORK

Photography by J & M Studio, New York

 POCKET BOOKS, a division of Simon & Schuster, Inc.
1230 Avenue of the Americas, New York, N.Y. 10020

ISBN: 0-671-54637-6

First Pocket Books printing March, 1985

10 9 8 7 6 5 4 3 2 1

Design by Stanley S. Drate/Folio Graphics Co., Inc.

*This book is dedicated
to the memory of a true friend,
James H. Hill,
who cannot be forgotten.
This one is for you, Jim.*

Acknowledgments

I would like to thank the following people for their never-ending assistance, advice, and encouragement. Without their help, this book would never have become a reality.

Paulette Vollheim
William H. Vollheim
Annemarie Vollheim
Eleanor Hill
Jonathan Hill
Mike Krinke
Jamie Hage
Susan Hage
T. J. Shaughnessy
David Therrien
René Therrien
J & M Studio

Preface

Airplanes have always fascinated me. Ever since I can remember, I have gone completely "ga-ga" over anything that flies. And over the years, I've found that when things get too hectic, or I have a problem to solve, designing and folding a paper airplane enables me to think clearly.

This book was written to provide the average person with paper airplane designs and techniques that actually work. I have experimented with most of the designs in this book since 1974, and have selected thirty that have been perfected. I hope you enjoy them.

The main purpose of this book is to provide you with an afternoon or evening of entertainment for just pennies. At a time when an air force, navy, or marine jet fighter costs from eight to thirty million dollars to build, you can create a whole air force for next to nothing. Using a few common household and office objects, you can make enough planes to declare yourself a third world nation if your imagination allows.

In this book, you will find designs for paper airplanes that can fly much better than the old favorites. Furthermore, many of the effective features found on the following designs—flaps, slats, winglets, etc.—can be incorporated into existing designs, yours or others.

MATERIALS

To make the airplanes in this book you need:
- 8½-by-11-inch paper (letter size)
- 8½-by-14-inch paper (legal size)
- 4" × 6" index cards
- business cards
- paper clips
- scissors
- plastic straws
- a razor blade
- cellophane tape
- a stapler
- a ruler

AERODYNAMICS

In order to help you understand why the planes in this book fly so well, I should touch on the subject of aerodynamics. Understanding the basic laws of aerodynamics will enable you to make paper airplanes with greater precision. Generally, there are four forces acting on an airplane at all phases of its flight.

The first is thrust, the forward motion of the plane through the air. The second is lift, which the wings produce as a result of forward motion. The third force—air resistance—is drag, which acts much like a sea anchor. The fourth force affecting a plane's flight is gravity. (Some people claim there is a fifth force—tail lift—but there is no one viewpoint on this controversial topic.) A quarter-ounce paper airplane and an 803,000-pound Boeing 747 are both affected by these principles.

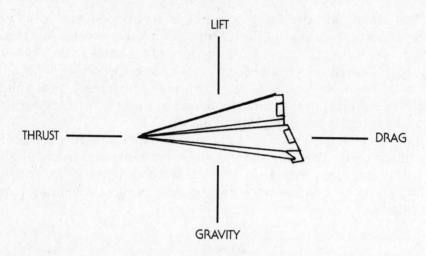

LIFT

THRUST

DRAG

GRAVITY

An airplane must also be properly balanced, having a correct center of gravity (CG). Every object has a center of gravity; that is, the point at which it will remain level if balanced. If you throw a pencil, for example, and it rotates end over end, the point around which it turns is the pencil's center of gravity. To obtain this correct CG, many of the airplanes in this book call for the addition of paper clips to the plane's nose. Design #14 needs four paper clips to give it a correct CG. This extra weight also increases the wing loading—the amount of weight the wings carry—or how hard the wings must work. If two airplanes weigh the same, but airplane A has half the wing area of airplane B, then airplane A has a higher wing loading. The wings on airplane A carry more weight. Generally, airplane A will have more stability because it is less affected by turbulence. But airplane A will also have a higher stall speed (which will be covered later).

The shape of a plane's airfoil (a cross-section of the wing), combined with thrust, is what gives a plane its lift. It is very hard to explain why these airfoils do produce lift. The best analogy I can come up with is to water coming out of a faucet. When the faucet is on low, you'll notice how the water stream is the same size as the hole in the spout as it leaves the faucet. But as the water nears the sink, the stream thins out, because the water is accelerating as gravity pulls it away from the faucet. Picture a "block" of air as it meets the forward, or leading edge of the airfoil. The "block" of air separates. Half of it goes over the top of the wing, while the other half goes under the wing.

SIDE VIEW OF WING

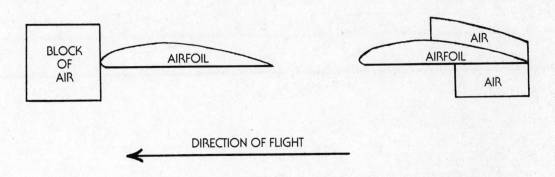

DIRECTION OF FLIGHT

This "block" of air must meet together at the trailing edge of the wing. Because the upper surface of the airfoil is curved, the top half of the block of air has a greater distance to travel than the lower half. Since the air on top of the airfoil has a greater distance to cover, it must speed up to arrive at the same time as the lower half. A high pressure airflow on the bottom of the wing is created, and a low pressure airflow on top, resulting in lift.

To understand the importance of airfoils, you must understand angle of attack. The angle of attack determines the speed of the airfoil through the air. The slower the wing speed, the greater the angle of attack required to maintain the same amount of lift—to keep the plane at the same altitude. The following example may help. After a water skier releases his two rope, he slows down, and the front of his skis must be raised in order to keep him on top of the water. However, as the skier raises his skis, more drag is created, slowing him down even more. He has to increase the angle again to compensate for this drag, which in turn creates more drag, etc., until the skis will no longer maintain the skier's weight. The same holds true for an airplane.

Different types of airfoils have different flying characteristics. While a thinner airfoil has less lift, it also has less drag because it has less air to displace. Though a thin wing is faster, it also will not maintain lift at as slow a speed as a thicker airfoil will. When an airfoil loses lift, a plane stalls. The airflow will not adhere to the top curved surface, eliminating all lift. This happens when the airfoil's angle of attack is too great.

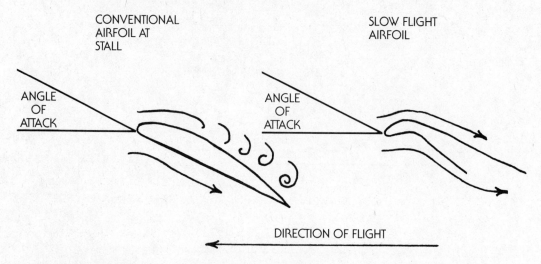

CONVENTIONAL
AIRFOIL AT
STALL

SLOW FLIGHT
AIRFOIL

ANGLE
OF
ATTACK

ANGLE
OF
ATTACK

DIRECTION OF FLIGHT

Design #2 (pp. 23–25) uses a terrific slow flight airfoil. This airfoil is basically a "paperized" version of NASA's Supercritical Airfoil, and flies very well at slow speeds. The plane appears to have no bad habits, which may have something to do with its delta-shaped wing, which in itself has stall-resistant characteristics.

Most of the designs in this book incorporate a differential stall wing—also referred to as "wash-out" or "wing twist"—first used by the late Jiro Horikoshi, designer of Japan's superior World War II Zero fighter. A differential stall wing's leading edge is twisted downward at the tips, either physically or aerodynamically. Physically, the wing tips are permanently twisted to reduce their angle of attack. Aerodynamically, leading edge slats (see below) effectively lessen the angle of attack, allowing the wing tips to generate lift at the stall phase. Since it is extremely difficult to physically make a conventional airfoil with a paper airplane, we can create this airfoil aerodynamically in the same way that a commercial airliner can modify its wings, to compensate for different flight requirements.

The designs in this book employ the aforementioned principles. The *leading* edge of the wing is dropped down, and acts like a shovel, scooping the airstream up and over the wing. These drooped leading wing edges are known as *slats*. As a rule, the *trailing* edge of the wing is folded down no more than 25% of the width of the wing to form *flaps*. These devices are used to:

14

increase lift; increase drag and rate of descent; reduce the stall speed; produce stability or instability depending on design; generally slow the airplane. The designs in this book use two types of flaps, hinged and split-type.

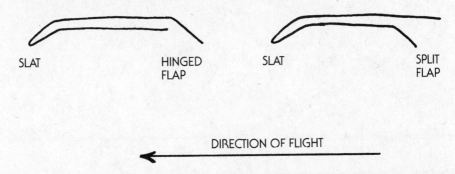

SLAT   HINGED   SLAT   SPLIT
                        FLAP   FLAP

DIRECTION OF FLIGHT

On full-sized aircraft, hinged flaps produce more lift than drag; split flaps produce more drag than lift. The reverse appears to be true with paper airplanes.

Now we come to *winglets,* which are playing quite an important role in today's "next generation" aircraft. Winglets are "end caps" for the wing. They help keep the air flowing across the wing instead of swirling around its tip, helping to prevent drag. Winglets prevent wingtip vortice (a swirling around the trailing wing tip which occurs because of the differences in air density or pressure that exist when a wing is in flight).

To prove that this effect is not limited only to large-scale aircraft, you can make a paper airplane of any design, make a cloud of cigar or cigarette smoke, and fly the airplane through the middle of the smoke cloud. You will notice how the smoke swirls around the wing tips. If you then cut and fold winglets and repeat the flight with the smoke cloud, you will actually see how much the swirling is reduced and is being converted to lift instead of drag.

Many of these designs employ inverted twin rudders, for stabilizing fins, which are located at the rear of the aircraft. Please note that the rudders are turned a few degrees inward to ensure stability. In addition, since the rudders are located at the wing tips, the inverted rudder also acts as a winglet, straightening out the airflow.

The dihedral angle is a subject all too often overlooked on a paper airplane. The dihedral angle is the angle at which the wings meet, and is paramount for stability. Most airplane wings are bent slightly upward. Increasing the wing's dihedral angle also increases the basic stability of the airplane by bringing the point of lift higher than or closer to the center of gravity. It also enables the aircraft to straighten itself out when deflected or rolled by wind or launching technique. When the airplane rolls, the upper wing loses lift due to its shorter lifting surface, while the lower wing increases in lifting surface, returning the airplane to level flight.

FRONT VIEW OF DESIGN #1

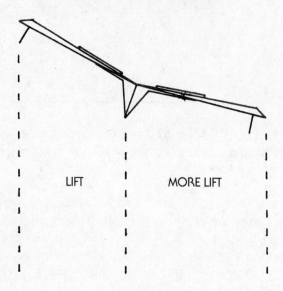

LIFT   MORE LIFT

TRIM

Trim is probably the most important facet of an airplane in flight. Due to the lift characteristics of the airfoil while in flight, the plane (full-sized or paper) has a tendency to dive, which increases its speed (which in turn makes the wing dive more). To counter this tendency in paper airplanes, the planes need *trim tabs*. By bending the tail of the plane upward slightly, you counteract the tendency to dive. How much trim you add will depend on trial and error. The more the trim tabs are raised, the higher the nose will want to be, thus creating a higher wing angle of attack, which in turn produces more lift; the airplane climbs, slowing down (much like a car coasting up hill). If you add flaps to the aircraft (especially split flaps if the design permits), some incredibly slow air speeds can be attained.

Do not be discouraged if your plane corkscrews and crashes on the first flight. Check to make sure that there is a slight dihedral angle, and make sure that pairs of leading edge slats, trim tabs (also called elevators), and rudders are bent at the same angle.

After a few days, or even a few flights, your planes will require retrimming. They tend to unfold and warp after a few hours, or after flying into a chair or wall.

If your airplane turns left or right, be *sure* that both wings match, and that the drooped leading edge of the wing, as well as the flaps (if you use them), are bent at the same angle. If your airplane still turns, you can slightly bend the outside rudder in the direction you want the airplane to go. For example, if the airplane turns left, bend the tail edge of the right rudder slightly to the right.

FINE TUNING

An airplane will have a flatter glide if it is aerodynamically clean. That is, nothing should disturb the airflow to cause drag. Keep your flap angles to a minimum. Spend an extra few minutes making your folds neat and crisp; the result is well worth the extra time.

FLYING WINGS

"Flying Wing" airplanes are truly fascinating. The concept behind them is that the plane's entire body—that which holds the wings and tail on a conventional airplane—can be eliminated, thereby reducing weight and drag. On a flying wing, the entire structure provides lift. Because of this great lift-over-drag ratio, flying-wing paper airplanes have an extremely flat glide. Flying wings, however, do not have a conventional stabilizing tail, and as a result, are unstable in turbulence (outdoor flying). They also tend to be extremely sensitive about center of gravity and trim, and are unstable if launched incorrectly.

In the late forties and early fifties, Northrop Corporation built several successful flying wing prototypes, the most noteworthy being a bomber called (oddly enough) "The Flying Wing." It was fast, could lift a large payload, and was clearly decades ahead of its time. Why it was never adopted by the armed forces, unfortunately, has to do with politics. Northrop was forced to destroy all flying wing prototypes. Today, NASA envisions the flying wing aircraft as the plane of the future, since it is incredibly efficient, combining a high load-carrying ability with speed.

CANARDS

My edition of *Webster's Dictionary* defines *canard* as "an airplane whose horizontal stabilizer is located forward of the wing or wings." Canard is also the French word for "duck," which appears to have its wings at the back end of its body. There are many advantages to this particular design, and few faults. A properly balanced conventional airplane requires a downward push on the tail to keep the airplane level (for example, nose-up trim tabs which push down the tail), which is counter-productive to achieving lift. In fact, this downward push is producing negative lift, creating drag. By moving the main wing back (which produces a nose-heavy craft), we can put a smaller wing in front that produces lift and helps the plane to stay level, eliminating induced drag. The smaller wing, or foreplane, is a productive stabilizer, whereas trim tabs of conventional craft are counter-productive (producing drag). Another advantage of the canard is that the drag that the main wing produces, which is considerable, is behind the center of gravity, which also helps to stabilize the airplane (much like a badminton shuttlecock). These designs also happen to be virtually stall-proof because as the angle of attack is increased, the foreplane (front wing), loses lift first, due to its design, airfoil, and size. When this happens, the nose drops, decreasing the angle of attack of both wings, eliminating any chance of a main wing stall. Thus, the canard is self-stabilizing.

The Wright brothers put the stabilizer in the front of their 1903 Wright Flyer, according to history, so that the pilot, who was positioned on the main wing, could keep a visual check on the position of the foreplane and eliminate the possibility of a pilot-induced stall. The stall at that time was still pretty much a mystery.

There is a very brilliant young airplane designer by the name of Burt Rutan, who at his Rutan Aircraft Factory headquarters has designed a series of full-sized canard aircraft and produces kits for canards that can be built in your own basement or garage. I have been lucky enough to fly one of these dynamic airplanes, and was very impressed with the superb handling, efficiency, safety, and high speed. To illustrate how well a canard or tandem-wing aircraft performs, one of Mr. Rutan's designs, a tandem-wing single-seat airplane named the "Quickie," has unbelievable performance: its cruise speed is 110 miles per hour. And at its cruise speed, it is getting 100 miles per gallon. All of this on a 22-horse-power engine.

The canard is an idea of the past, but clearly it is also a design of the future. Mr. Rutan and the Rutan Aircraft Factory have given birth to a new generation of designs.

GENERAL INSTRUCTIONS FOR FOLDING

This is the part of the book that counts: the airplanes. If you have read this far, you have done your homework, and now it's time to fly. The following are some general rules:

- All of the construction phases are shown with the airplane pointed to the left.
- Where a fold is indicated (dotted lines), *make a mirror image fold on the other side.* Where a cut is indicated (solid lines), make the cut through to the other side. In this manner the features are identical on both wings.
- I suggest starting with design #1, and progressing numerically through to #30.
- All the designs have been photographed after flight testing (note: some have wrinkled noses), so you have a guide for folding and trim. All fly well as shown.
- The dimensions of the leading edge slats, flaps, rudders, and trim tabs (elevators) are not critical, but countless stacks of paper and many hours have helped me determine that these are best.

LAUNCHING

Obviously, these paper airplanes are all gliders. They have to convert altitude into forward speed in order to fly once they leave your hand. Therefore, you should launch them with the nose down slightly for indoor flying, with a gentle but sure motion—more of a push than a throw. For outdoor flying, any technique works.

Airplanes that are flown outdoors require more speed to overcome turbulence, so they do not require as much nose-up trim as indoor airplanes. For airplanes that are used for distance or endurance flights, I usually do not use flaps, as this will almost always shorten the plane's glide distance. The longest flight I have ever experienced from ground-level launching was twenty eight seconds, with design #3.

Standard launching technique for a conventional design

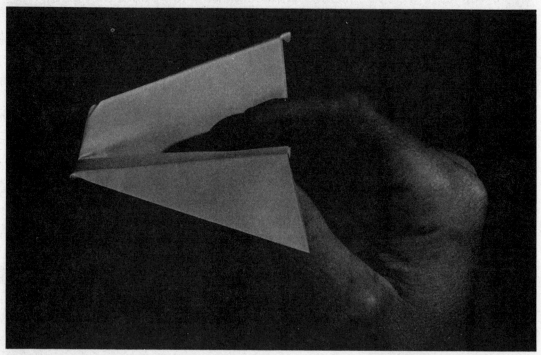

Standard launching technique for a flying wing

Standard launching technique for a canard

DESIGN *1*

This one was the first design I experimented with, and looks quite like "your basic world-known paper airplane." It is the basis for planes #2 through #6 as well as the modified slow flyers that appear at the end of this book. Design #1 is good for indoor as well as outdoor flying, and has excellent slow as well as fast flight characteristics. This is a good airplane for "high apartment window" flying.

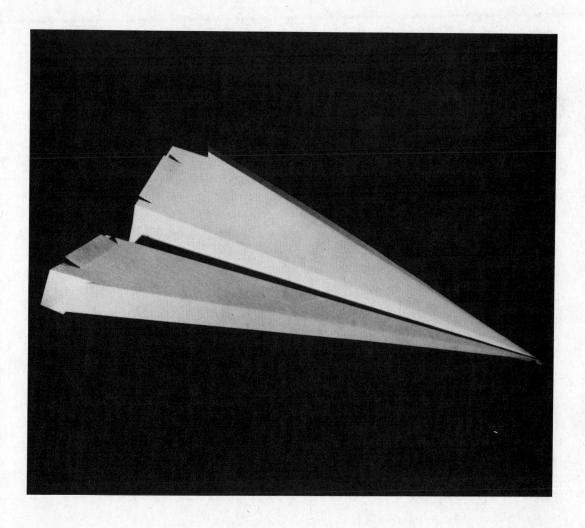

one 8½-by-11-inch piece of paper
ruler
scissors or razor blade
tape

1a). Fold 8½-by-11-inch paper in half lengthwise.

1b). Fold corners to the outside.

1c). Fold paper left corner to match bottom fold, and measure 1¼″ from the bottom at the trailing edge.

1d). Fold wings along a diagonal line from 1¼" mark at rear to the nose.

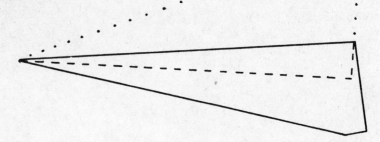

1e). Unfold wings. Using a scissor or razor blade, make two ½" cuts at the trailing edge and make a 1" cut at the wing tip, in the approximate locations in the sketch. Tape center section.

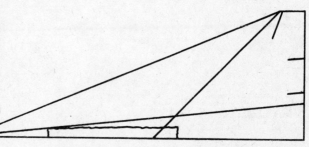

1f). Fold down rudders, note folded angle. Fold down leading edge slat about ⅝" at the tip.

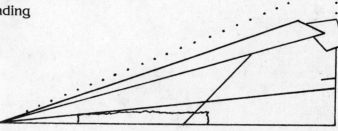

1g). Unfold the leading edge slats and rudders (see photograph). Bend the elevators at the trailing edge slightly upward.

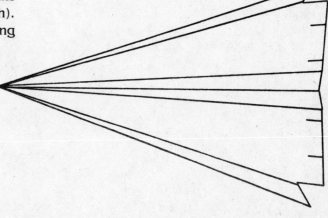

DESIGN 2

At a quick glance, this design appears to be the same as #1. Basically, it is, except that it uses the slow flight airfoil. This is an excellent airplane for indoors or out, and does well under windy conditions. It is extremely stable and can be slowed to a crawl without any extra lift-producing devices.

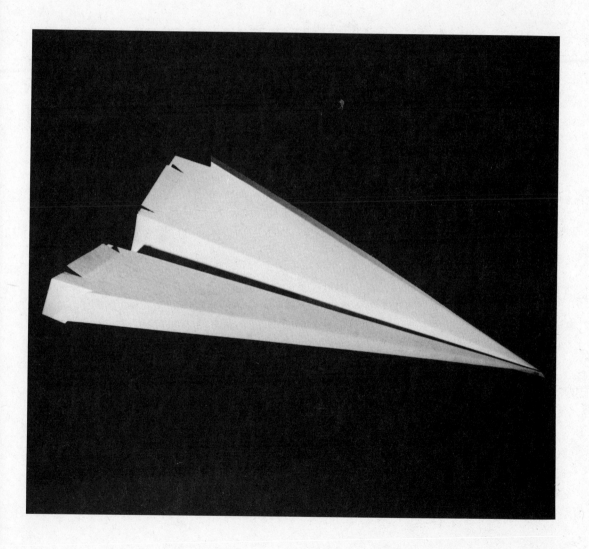

REQUIRED: one 8½-by-11-inch piece of paper
ruler
scissors or razor blade
tape

2a). Follow steps 1a through 1f.

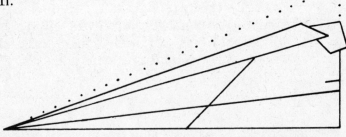

2b). Pull center section down ⅜"
and tape. Cut off excess tape. See
photo on next page.

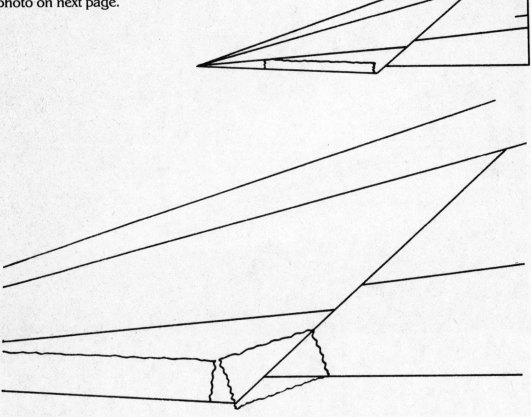

28

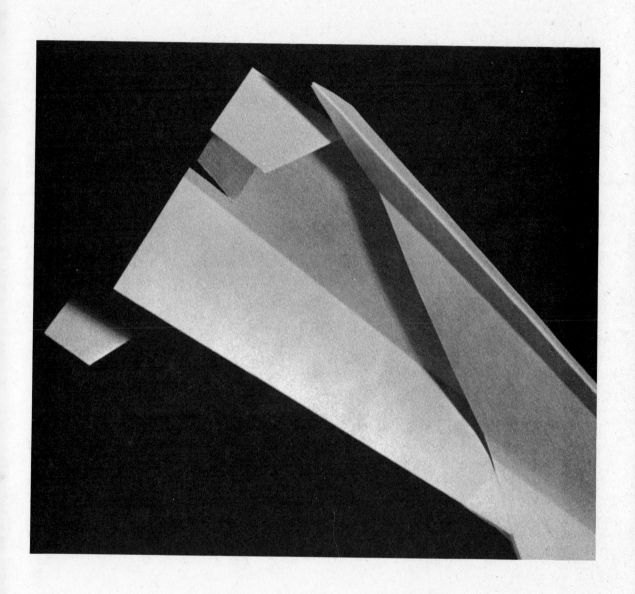

DESIGN 3

This is one of my favorites. It is an excellent, stable, outdoor flyer. When trimmed properly, it will turn into the wind and hover. This design uses flaps that can also be used on designs #1, #2, #4, #8, #10, #12, and #14.

REQUIRED: one 8½-by-11-inch piece of paper
ruler
razor blade
tape

3a). Follow steps 1a through 1c. Fold leading edge of wing to match bottom fold.

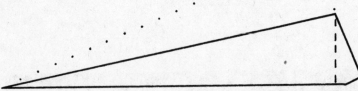

3b). Unfold wings. Using a razor blade, make ½" cuts for elevators and flaps. When cutting flaps, make sure you cut through both wings. Cut rudders. Tape center section.

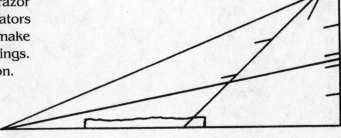

3c). Fold rudders. Fold leading edge slats ⅝", as in previous designs.

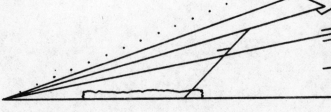

3d). Unfold airplane and fold leading edge slat in half again. Fold flaps in the approximate position in the photograph below.

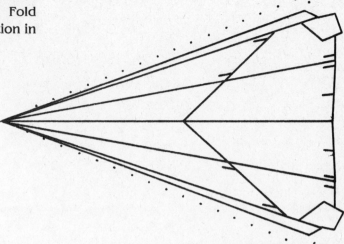

DESIGN 4

This plane is reminiscent of the Concord SST, and is very stable at high speed. It will "Dutch Roll," or ossilate if allowed too much angle of attack (too much nose-up trim). It should look like a flattened "W" when viewed from the nose or tail. This design also uses the central inverted "V" rudder, which provides a limited amount of nose-up trim. It is important that the slats be flattened so that there is only a slight droop. This design requires one paper clip on the nose to acquire a proper CG.

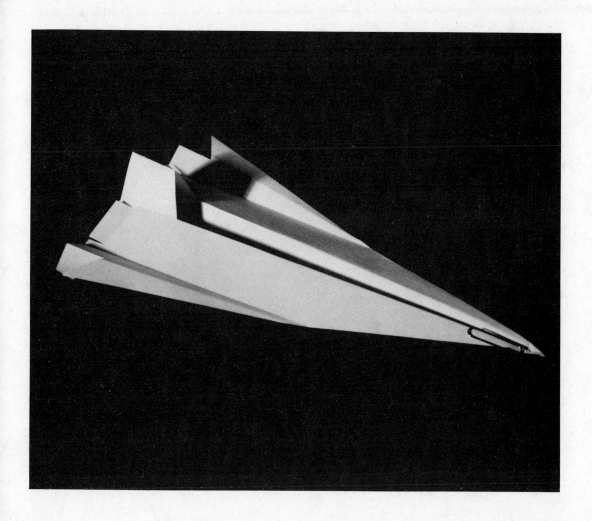

REQUIRED: one 8½-by-11-inch piece of paper
ruler
scissors or razor blade
tape
one paper clip

4a). Follow steps 1a through 1d. Fold wings up according to sketch.

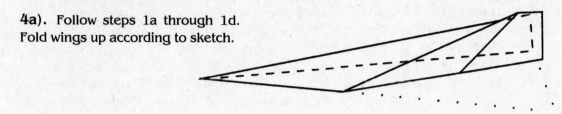

4b). Cut along lines, and tape center section.

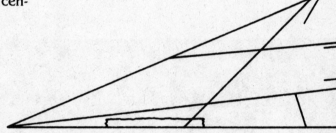

4c). Fold down rudders and fold leading edge slats only to the fold at the mid-wing point. Fold central inverted "V" rudder up as shown. Attach paper clip to the nose.

DESIGN 5

This is a very stable, stall-proof, docile bird, and a favorite of mine. The wing is a little weak. If you tape or glue the leading edge slats together delicately, however, it will be considerably stronger.

REQUIRED: one 8½-by-11-inch piece of paper
scissors or razor blade
tape
one paper clip

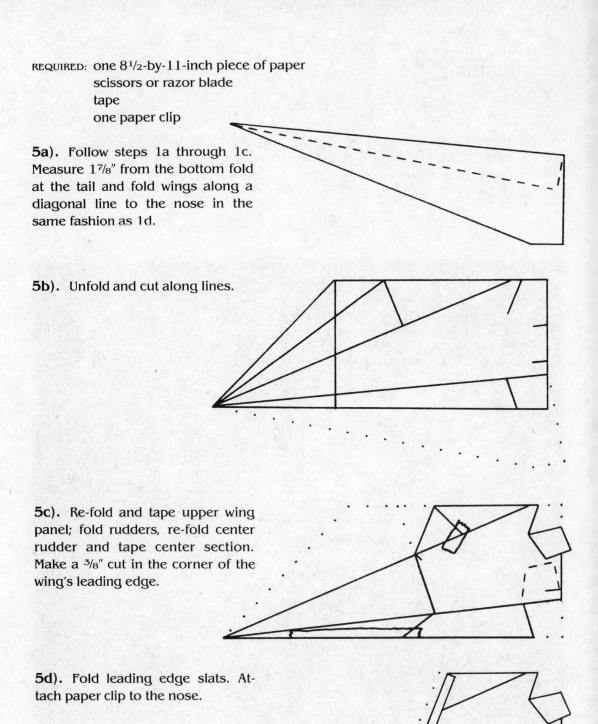

5a). Follow steps 1a through 1c. Measure 1⅞" from the bottom fold at the tail and fold wings along a diagonal line to the nose in the same fashion as 1d.

5b). Unfold and cut along lines.

5c). Re-fold and tape upper wing panel; fold rudders, re-fold center rudder and tape center section. Make a ⅜" cut in the corner of the wing's leading edge.

5d). Fold leading edge slats. Attach paper clip to the nose.

DESIGN 6

This is a canard. For nose-up trim, the elevators on the front wing are bent *down*. It is quite stable.

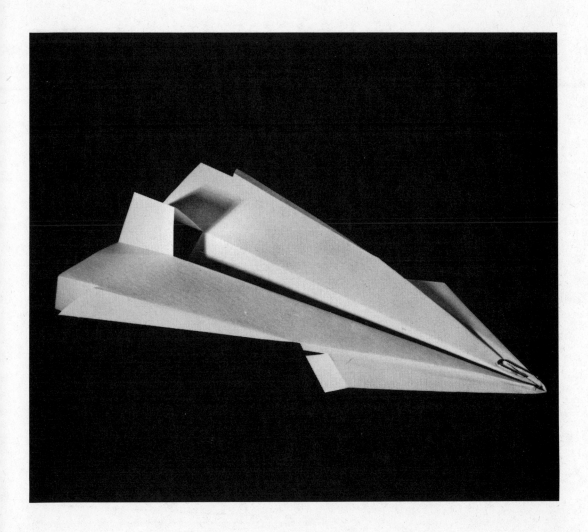

REQUIRED: one 8½-by-11-inch piece of paper
ruler
scissors or razor blade
tape
one paper clip

6a). Follow steps 1a through 1d. Unfold insides as shown.

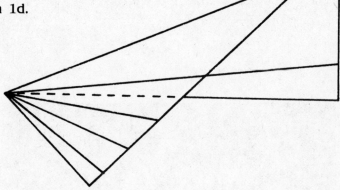

6b). Turn plane upside down as shown.

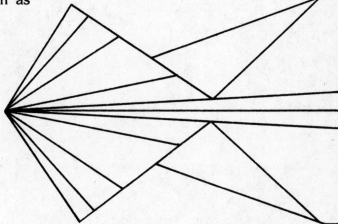

6c). Fold and tape as shown.

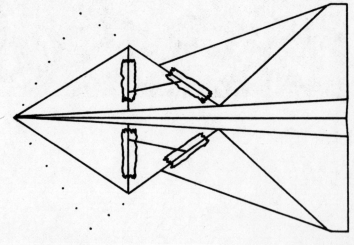

6d). Cut rudders and elevator on front wing. Tape according to sketch.

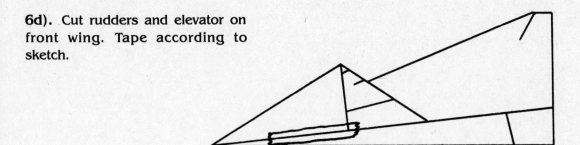

6e). Fold rudders down, as well as leading edge slats on the main, or rear, wing. Fold center rudder up. Attach a paper clip to the nose.

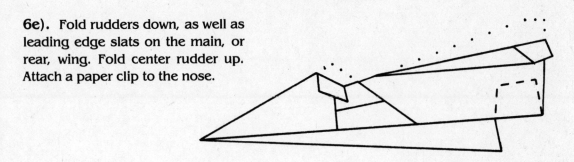

DESIGN 7

This is a semi-canard, using the canard stabilizing wing as well as conventional elevators. Though it is stable, it has an excellent turning radius.

REQUIRED: one 8½-by-11-inch piece of paper
ruler
tape
scissors or razor blade
two paper clips

7a). Fold 8½-by-11-inch paper 3″ widthwise.

7b). Fold bottom up to meet top and fold wings so approximately ³⁄₄″ is left unfolded at each end.

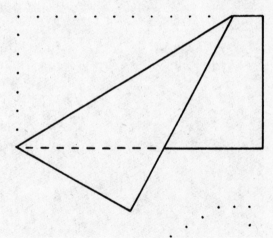

7c). Measure 1¼″ from bottom fold at the tail, fold wings along this line to the nose.

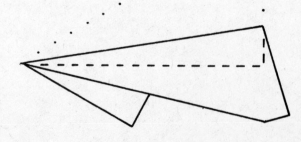

7d). Unfold wings, cut rudders, center rudder. Cut elevators approximately ½". Tape according to sketch.

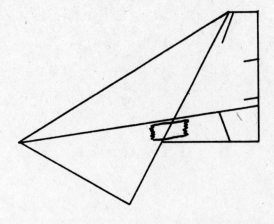

7e). Fold rudders down, fold center rudder up. Fold foreplane slat down approximately ⅜".

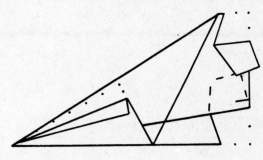

7f). Fold slats on main wing. Attach two paper clips to the nose.

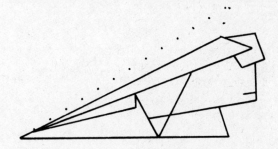

DESIGN 8

This is a good flyer, usually requiring little or no nose-up trim. Split flaps can be used. Excellent for "high apartment window" flying. One paper clip can be added to the nose for better wind penetration during outdoor flights.

REQUIRED: one 8½-by-11-inch piece of paper
ruler
scissors or razor blade
tape

8a). Follow steps 1a through 1b. Unfold, except corners. With folded corners facing up, fold over.

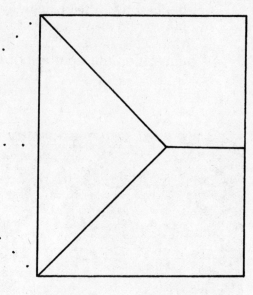

8b). Re-fold in half lengthwise.

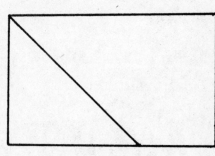

8c). Fold corners as shown.

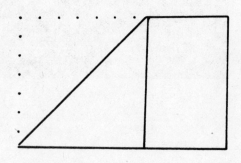

8d). Measure 1¼″ from the bottom fold at the tail and fold wings along diagonal line to nose.

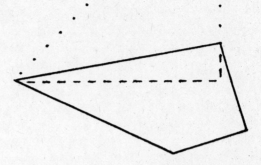

8e). Cut along lines shown. Tape center section.

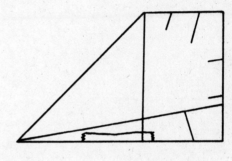

8f). Fold rudders, winglets, and leading edge slats.

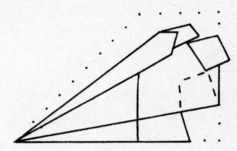

DESIGN 9

This is a semi-flying wing. It has an extremely flat glide. Trimming is accomplished by varying the fold angle of the leading edge slats. Flatten them out for more nose-up trim, fold them down for more nose-down trim.

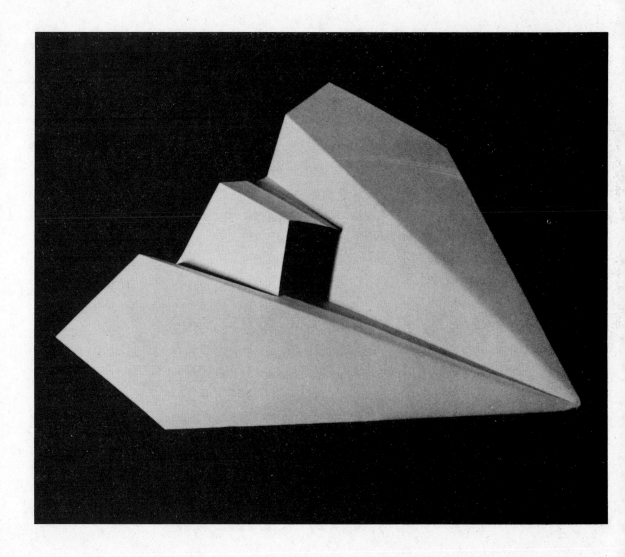

REQUIRED: one 8½-by-11-inch piece of paper
ruler
scissors or razor blade
tape

9a). Follow steps 8a through 8c. Cut center rudder approximately a 1¼″ cut as shown.

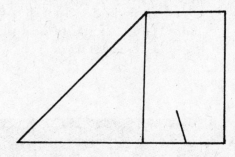

9b). Fold center rudder up, note slight upward angle. Final trim adjustment can also be accomplished by re-folding the center rudder at different angles. Tape center section.

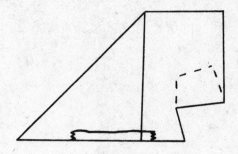

9c). Fold leading edge slats down to match bottom fold.

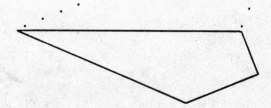

DESIGN *10*

This is an extremely stable airplane, usually requiring no nose-up trim. This plane is similar in looks to an F4 Phantom. Paper clips can be added to the nose for better wind penetration. This one is excellent for indoor flying or "high apartment window" flying.

REQUIRED: One 8½-by-11-inch piece of paper
ruler
scissors or razor blade
tape
up to four paper clips (optional)

10a). Follow steps 8a through 8c. Measure 1¼″ from the bottom fold at the tail and fold wings along diagonal line to nose

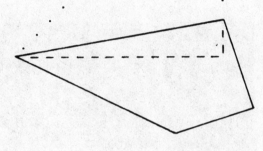

10b). Fold wings up to match top fold.

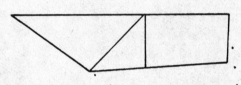

10c). Cut rudders, winglets, elevators, center rudder, and slats. Tape center section.

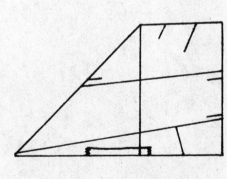

10d). Fold center and wingtip rudders, winglets, and leading edge slats as shown. Attach paper clips to nose.

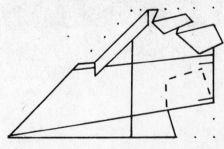

This is a true flying wing, having no stabilizing tail. Trimming is accomplished by folding the leading edge slats in the same manner as in design #9.

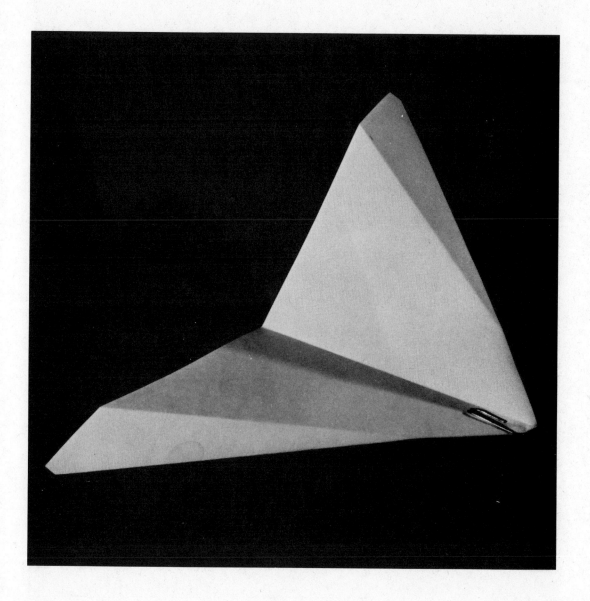

REQUIRED: one 8½-by-11-inch piece of paper
          ruler
          tape
          one paper clip

11a). Fold 8½-by-1-inch paper in half widthwise.

11b). Fold corners as shown.

11c). Lay flat and fold point to corner edge.

11d). Fold in half.

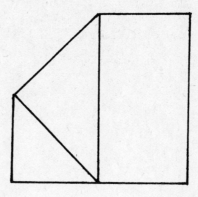

11e). Fold edges back, and tape as shown.

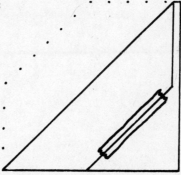

11f). Two inches from the nose, start folding the leading edge slat as shown. Add one paper clip to the nose.

DESIGN *12*

This is very similar to #10, but has less wing area, and, as a result, has a slightly shorter glide. This is an excellent "high apartment window" flyer.

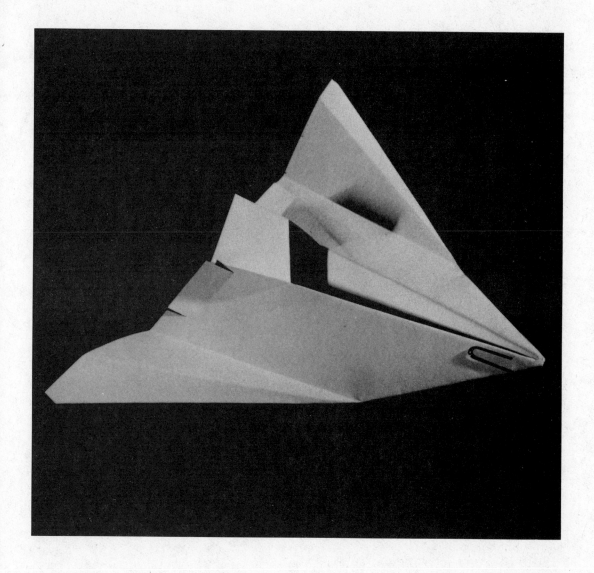

REQUIRED: 8½-by-11-inch piece of paper
ruler
scissors or razor blade
tape
one paper clip

12a). Follow steps 11a through 11e. Measure 1¼″ from the bottom fold at the tail and fold wings along line to nose.

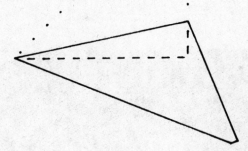

12b). Fold wings up approximately 1″ over the top.

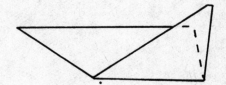

12c). Unfold wings and cut center rudder and elevators. Tape center section as shown.

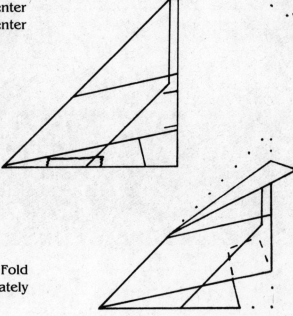

12d). Fold up center rudder. Fold leading edge slats approximately ⅝″. Attach paper clip to nose.

This one flys very well indoors as well as outdoors. It has a large wing area and can be launched briskly.

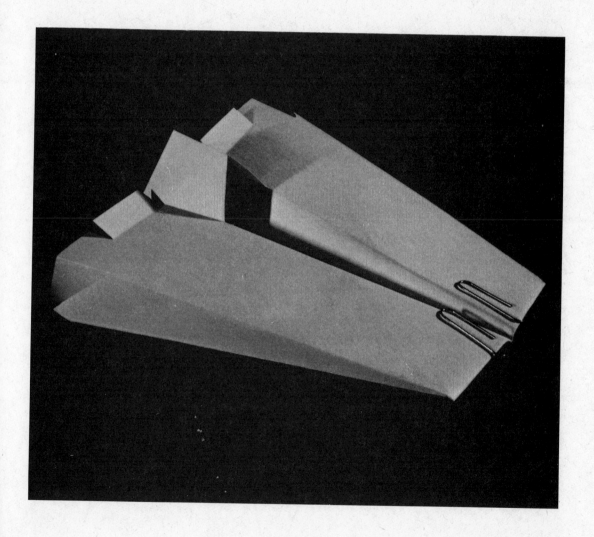

REQUIRED: one 8½-by-11-inch piece of paper
ruler
scissors or razor blade
tape
two paper clips

13a). Follow steps 1a through 1c. Unfold wings. Measure 2″ from trailing edge. Fold point to it.

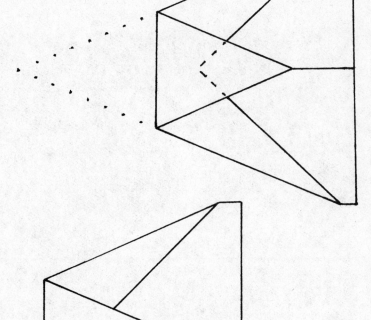

13b). Fold in half.

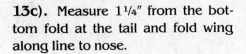

13c). Measure 1¼″ from the bottom fold at the tail and fold wing along line to nose.

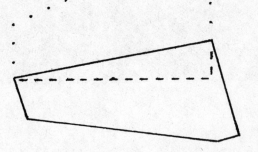

13d). Unfold wings and cut rudders, elevators, and center rudder. Tape according to sketch.

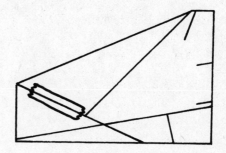

13e). Fold central rudder, rudders, and slats as shown. Attach paper clips to nose.

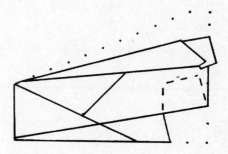

DESIGN 14

This one is a little gem. It has a high wing loading (it has a small wing for its weight). Excellent for outdoors as well as indoors, it has a high glide speed. It requires a fine hand in trimming.

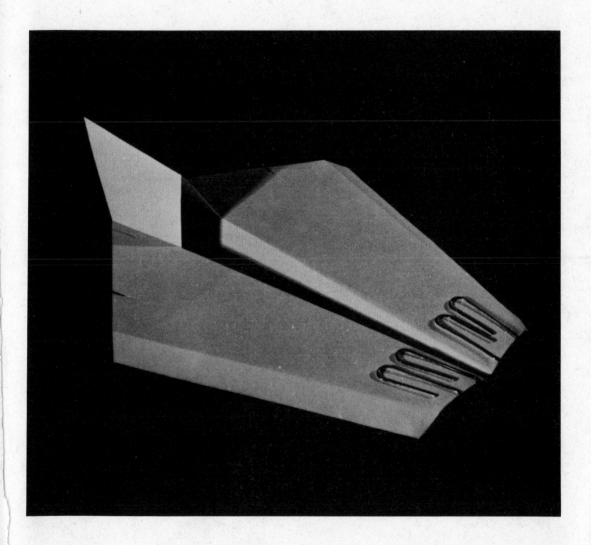

REQUIRED: One 8½-by-11-inch piece of paper (cut down to 8½″ × 8½″)
tape
ruler
scissors or razor blade
four paper clips

14a). Cut an 8½-by-11-inch piece
of paper to 8½″ × 8½″ square and
fold diagonally.

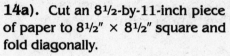

14b). Fold leading edges as
shown.

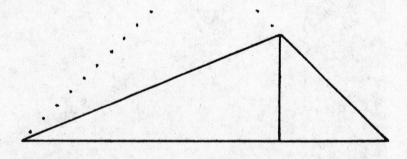

14c). Lay flat and fold point back,
as shown, to meet fold.

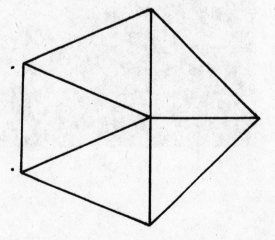

14d). Fold in half (folding bottom wing underneath wing tip) and tape center section.

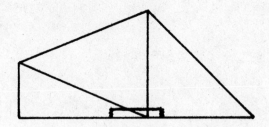

14e). Measure 1¼″ from the bottom of the fold at the tail, fold to nose.

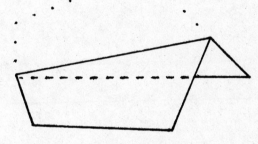

14f). Unfold wings. Cut center rudder and elevators.

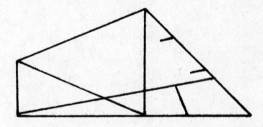

14g). Fold center rudder up, fold slats down approximately ½″. Attach paper clips to nose.

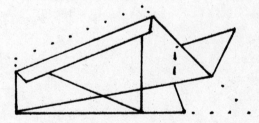

DESIGN 15

This semi-flying wing is restricted to indoor or "high apartment window" flying. Trimming is done in the same manner as #9 and #11.

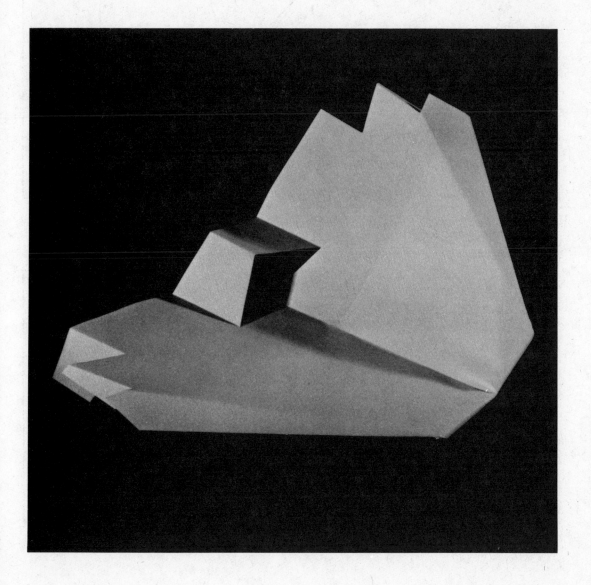

REQUIRED: one 8½-by-11-inch piece of paper
scissors or razor blade
tape

15a). Fold 8½-by-11-inch piece of
paper diagonally as shown.

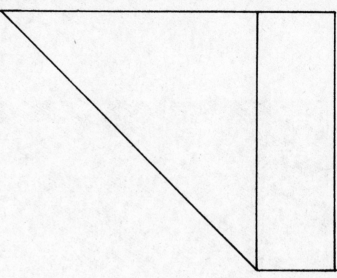

15b). Unfold and fold other corner
as shown.

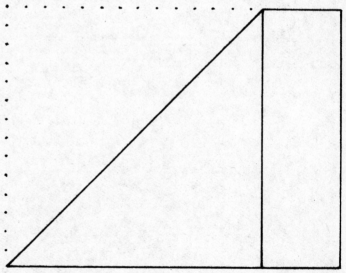

15c). Unfold again and tuck in sides while folding over top as shown.

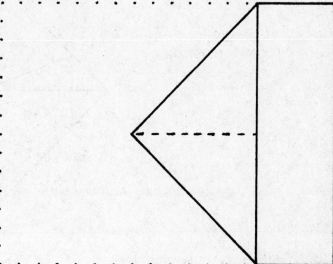

15d). Forward view of step 15c.

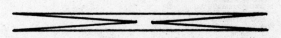

15e). Fold the top folds up to meet the nose.

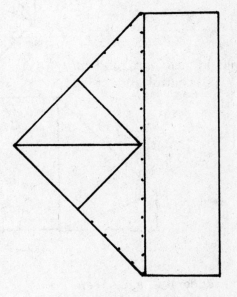

15f). Fold top folds to meet center, as shown.

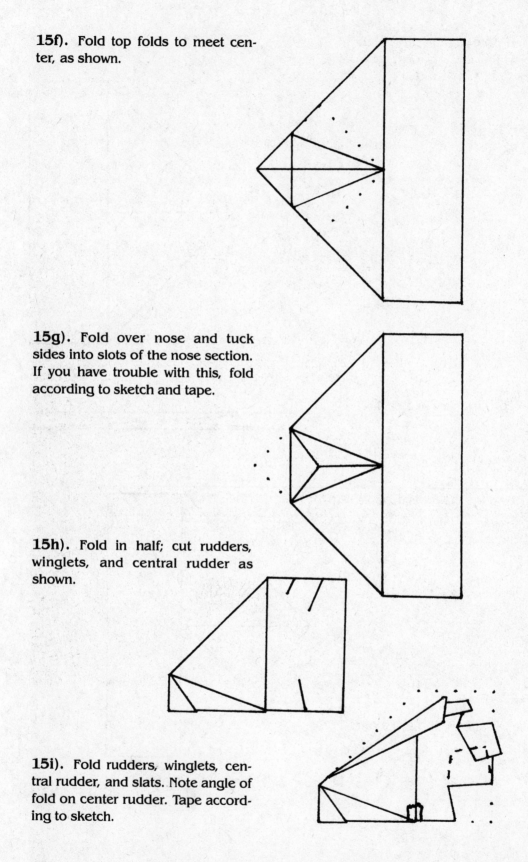

15g). Fold over nose and tuck sides into slots of the nose section. If you have trouble with this, fold according to sketch and tape.

15h). Fold in half; cut rudders, winglets, and central rudder as shown.

15i). Fold rudders, winglets, central rudder, and slats. Note angle of fold on center rudder. Tape according to sketch.

DESIGN *16*

This is a simple flying wing. No trimming is necessary, and, considering its simple form, it flies exceptionally well.

REQUIRED one 8½-by-11-inch piece of paper (cut down to 8½" × 8½")
scissors or razor blade
ruler
tape
one paper clip

16a). Cut an 8½-by-11-inch piece of paper to 8½" × 8½" square and fold diagonally.

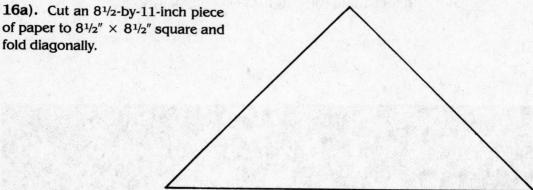

16b). Fold wings as shown.

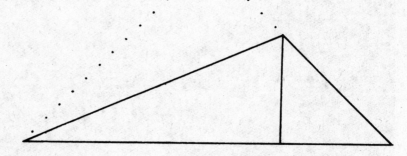

16c). Lay flat and fold point back as shown, to meet fold.

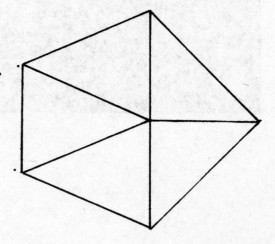

16d). Fold back leading edge 1½″ and tape according to sketch.

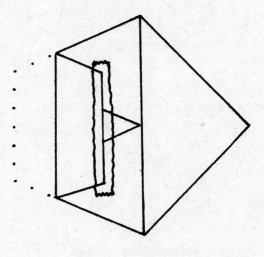

16e). Fold in half. Fold slats about ⅜″. Attach paper clip to nose.

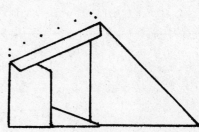

DESIGN 17

This is a true flying wing. It features an extremely flat glide if trimmed properly. Trimming is done by the same method used in designs #9, #11, and #15. It is quite sensitive to trim deployment.

REQUIRED: one 8½-by-11-inch piece of paper (cut down to 8½″ × 8½″)
scissors or razor blade
tape

17a). Cut an 8½-by-11-inch piece of paper to 8½″ × 8½″ square and fold diagonally.

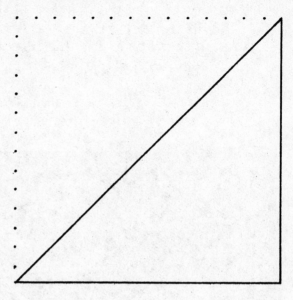

17b). Unfold and fold other corner as shown.

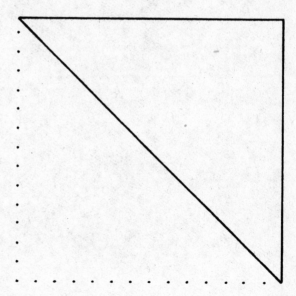

17c). Unfold again and tuck in sides while folding over top, as shown.

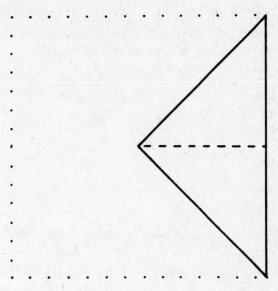

17d). Forward view of step 17c.

17e). Fold the top folds up to meet the nose.

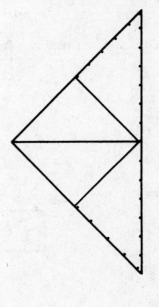

17f). Fold top folds to meet at center, as shown.

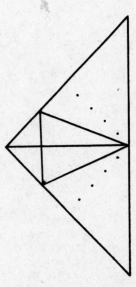

17g). Fold over nose and tuck sides into slots of the nose section. If you have trouble with this, fold according to sketch and tape.

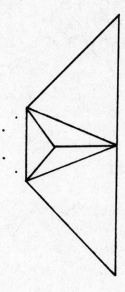

17h). Fold in half as shown, bringing bottom half under top half.

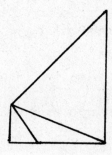

17i). Fold according to sketch.

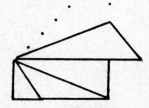

DESIGN *18*

This is an extremely stable and fast airplane. Perfect for just about any conditions, it has a high wing loading and can be launched briskly.

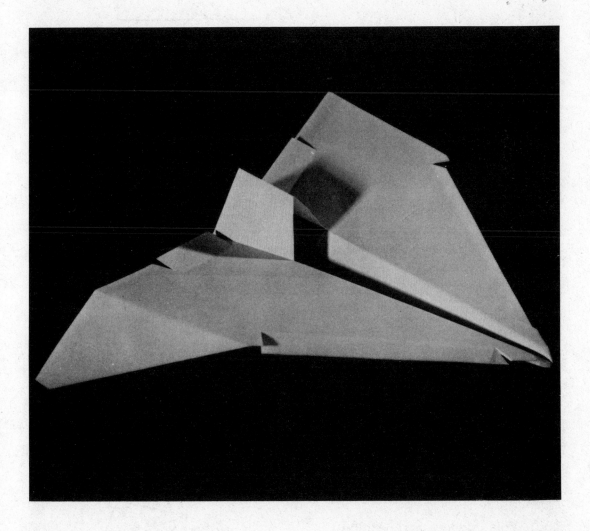

REQUIRED: one 8½-by-11-inch piece of paper
ruler
scissors or razor blade
tape

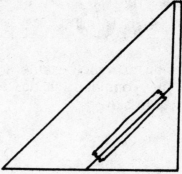

18a). Follow steps 11a through 11e.

18b). Measure 1¼" from the tail and fold wings along line to nose.

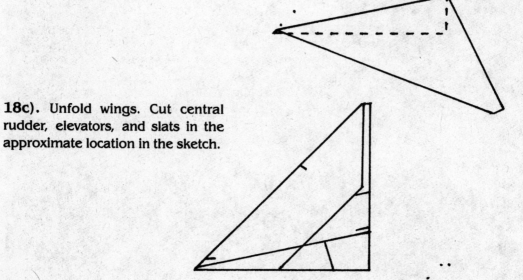

18c). Unfold wings. Cut central rudder, elevators, and slats in the approximate location in the sketch.

18d). Fold rudders and leading edge slats down, and central rudder up.

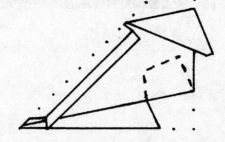

DESIGN *19*

This one is an excellent flyer. It can also be made in proportionally smaller sizes. Keep leading edge slat bend to a minimum—too much and the plane becomes unstable. #19 exhibits a flat glide.

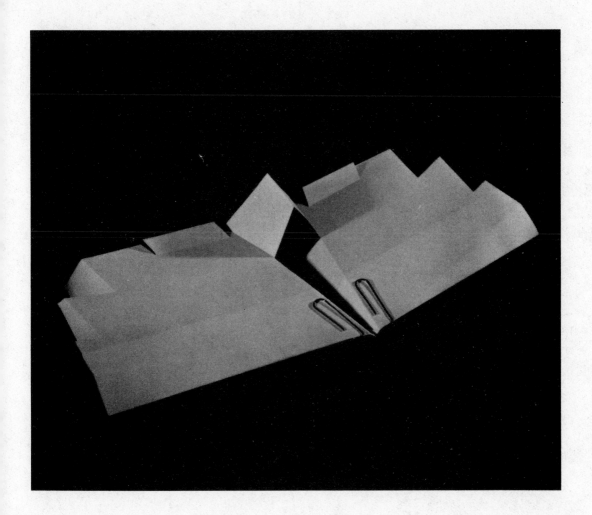

REQUIRED: One 8½-by-11-inch piece of paper
         tape
         ruler
         scissors or razor blade
         two paper clips

19a). Fold top of 8½-by-11-inch
piece of paper lengthwise.

19b). Fold top again (in half
lengthwise) to meet first edge, tape.

19c). Turn paper 90° to the left. Fold in half, bottom half under top half.

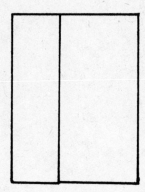

19d). Measure 1¼″ from the bottom fold at the tail and fold wings along line to nose.

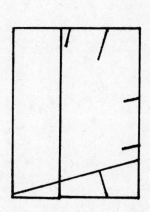

19e). Unfold wings, and cut rudders, winglets, elevators, and central rudder.

19f). Fold central rudder up, winglets and rudders down, and slats according to sketch. Attach two paper clips to the nose.

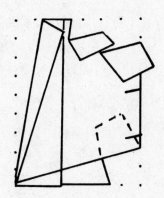

DESIGN *20*

This is basically design #19 with an inverted gull wing. This feature enhances stability dramatically.

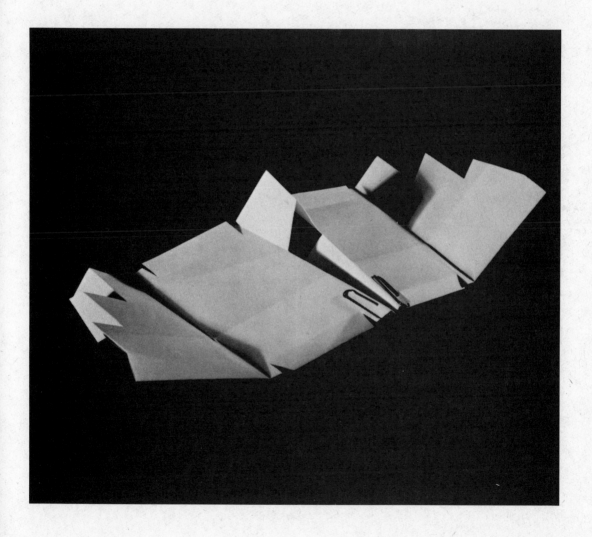

REQUIRED: one 8½-by-11-inch piece of paper
tape
ruler
scissors or razor blade
two paper clips

20a). Follow steps 19a through 19b. Fold wings up to approximate position shown in sketch.

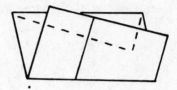

20b). Unfold wings. Cut rudders, winglets, central rudder, and slats, according to sketch.

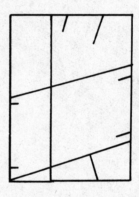

20c). Fold central rudder, winglets, slats, and rudders. Attach two paper clips to the nose.

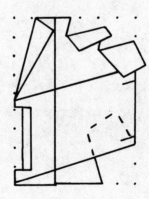

DESIGN 21

This is a gentle flyer, excellent for "high apartment window" flying. Keep leading edge slat bend to a minimum.

REQUIRED: One 8½-by-14-inch piece of paper
         ruler
         tape
         scissors or razor blade
         stapler

21a). Fold 8½-by-14-inch piece of
paper in half widthwise.

21b). Fold corners as shown.

21c). Fold the nose over 2″ as shown.

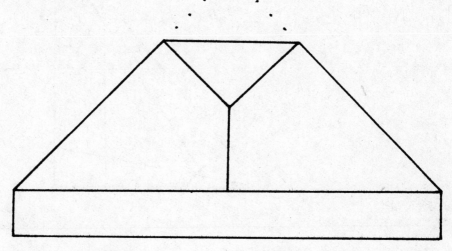

21d). Re-fold in half, bottom half under top half. Fold leading edges back to the approximate position shown in the sketch and tape.

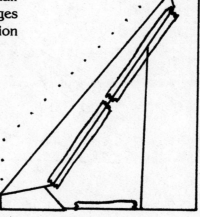

21e). Measure 1¼″ from the bottom fold at the tail and fold wings along line to nose.

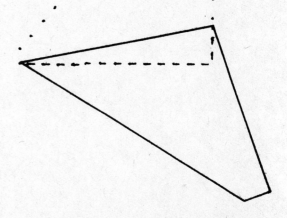

21f). Cut central rudder, elevators, and rudders.

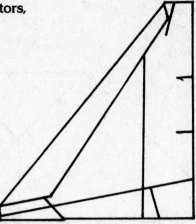

21g). Fold central rudder up, rudders down, and slats down approximately ⅝″. Staple nose together under wings.

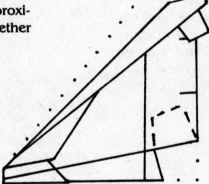

DESIGN 22

This is a curious flying airplane. It glides with a series of ossilations due to its weak wing. Because of its weak structure, it has to be launched with a negative dihedral angle, which will enable it to flex to a slight dihedral in flight.

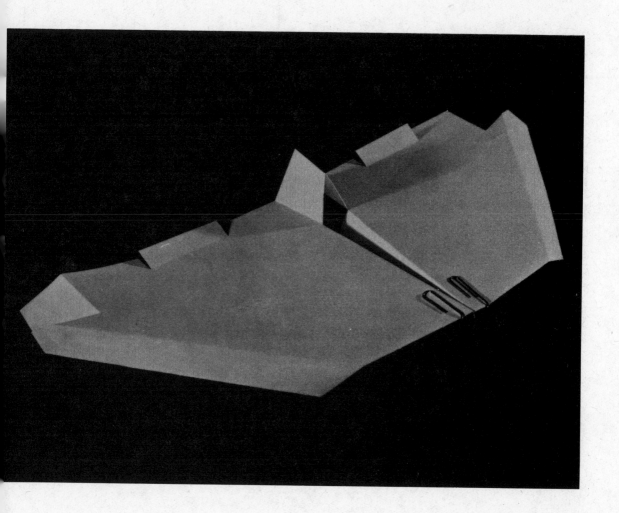

one 8½-by-14-inch piece of paper
tape
ruler
scissors or razor blade
two paper clips
stapler

22a). Fold an 8½-by-14-inch piece of paper in half widthwise.

22b). Fold corners as shown.

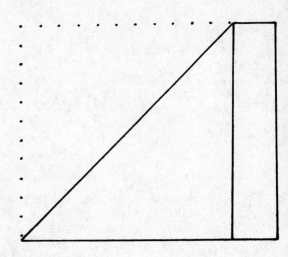

22c). Unfold and fold point back as shown.

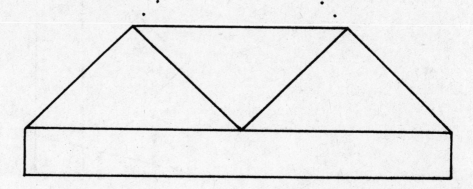

22d). Fold paper in half, bottom half under top half, and tape center section.

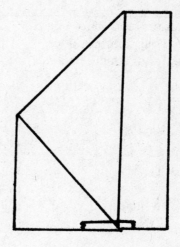

22e). Measure 1¼″ from the bottom fold at the tail and fold wings along line to nose.

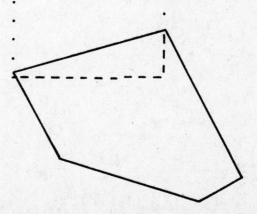

22f). Cut central rudder, elevators and rudders.

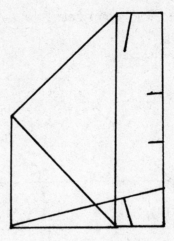

22g). Fold rudders and slats approximately $5/8''$. Fold central rudder up. Staple nose and attach paper clips to nose.

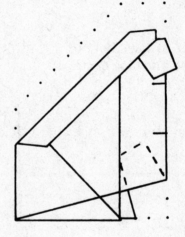

DESIGN 23

This design features a fast glide due to its high wing loading. Since it is so small, it is sensitive to folding errors. A good plane for indoors or outdoors, it can be launched briskly.

REQUIRED: one 4″ × 6″ index card
ruler
scissors or razor blade
three paper clips

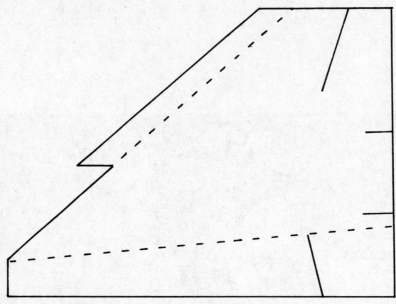

Full-Size Pattern

23a). Fold 4″ × 6″ index card in half widthwise. Trace the design above, making sure to align fold with bottom of pattern. Cut according to pattern.

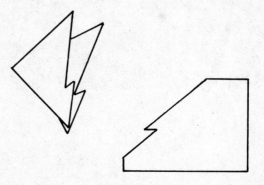

23b). Measure ³/₄″ from the bottom fold at the tail and ³/₈″ from the nose and fold wings along diagonal line.

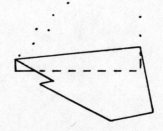

23c). Cut rudders and elevators.

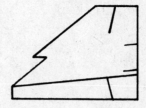

23d). Fold rudders and leading edge slats. Attach three paper clips to the nose.

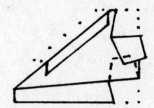

DESIGN *24*

This is a fast gliding airplane, due to its high wing loading. With the wing tips folded down, doubling as rudders and winglets, this is a more efficient design than #23, even though it carries an extra paper clip for stability, resulting in more weight.

REQUIRED: one 4″ × 6″ index card
scissors or razor blade
four paper clips

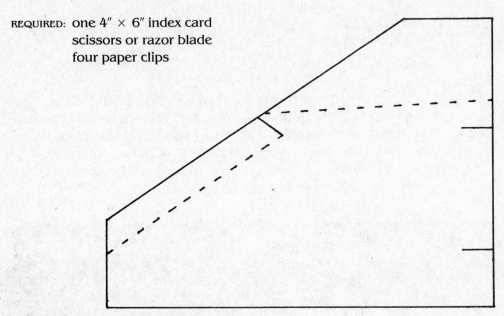

Full-Size Pattern

24a). Fold 4″ × 6″ index card in half widthwise. Trace the design above, making sure to align fold with bottom of pattern. Cut according to pattern.

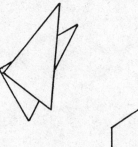

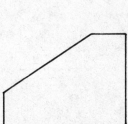

24b). Cut elevators and slats.

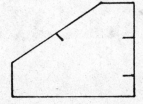

24c). Fold rudder/winglets and slats. Attach four paper clips to the nose.

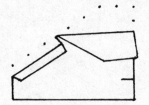

DESIGN 25

This one is probably the most efficient design in this book, requiring no paper clips to obtain a correct CG. It illustrates the true efficiency of a canard. This airplane will fly with very little trim, and at a five-degree nose-up attitude. The foreplane should have a pronounced negative dihedral (or anhedral), while the main wing should have the standard dihedral.

REQUIRED: one 8½-by-5½-inch piece of paper
one 2″ × 3½″ business card, or equivalent
scissors or razor blade
tape
ruler
one plastic straw

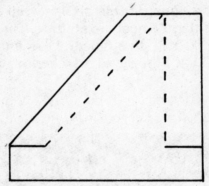

Full-Size Foreplane Pattern

25a). Fold 8½-by-5½-inch piece of paper in half widthwise. Fold 2″ × 3½″ business card in half widthwise as well. On the business card, trace the design above, making sure to align fold with bottom of pattern. Cut according to pattern.

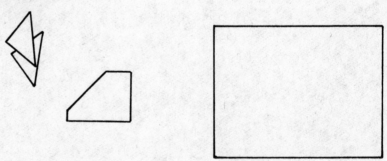

25b). Fold corners of the paper as shown, and cut leading edge slats and elevators on business card.

25c). Cut rudders on main wing and fold slats on foreplane (business card). Tape center section on main wing.

25d). Fold rudders and leading edge slats on main wing approximately ⅝". Fold foreplane to negative dihedral (down) and fold elevators down.

25e). Tape the foreplane on top of the straw, as shown. Then tape the straw exactly 2" back from the main wing's leading point.

DESIGN 26

This design was conceived for a canard with a little more wing area and a little more weight than design #25—for wind penetration for outdoor flying. As with all canards, it is extremely stable.

REQUIRED: one 8½-by-5½-inch piece of paper
one 4″ × 6″ index card
scissors or razor blade
tape
one plastic straw
ruler
one paper clip

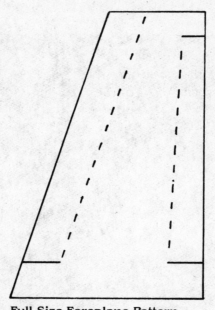

Full-Size Foreplane Pattern

26a). Fold 8½-by-5½-inch piece of paper and 4″ × 6″ index card in half widthwise. On the index card, trace design above, making sure to align fold with bottom of pattern. Cut according to pattern.

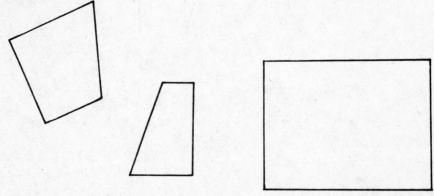

26b). Fold corners on main wing, as shown. Cut leading edge slats and elevators on foreplane as well as rudder on main wing.

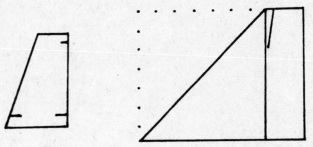

26c). Fold rudders and slats approximately ⅝" on main wing. Fold slats on foreplane. Tape center section on main wing.

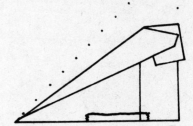

26d). Tape the foreplane on top of the straw. Tape the straw on top of the main wing, 2" back from the wing's leading point. Attach paper clip to nose.

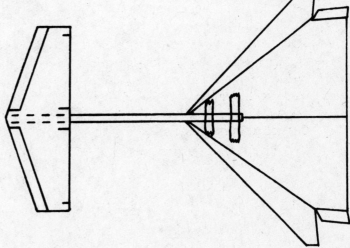

DESIGN 27

This canard has a higher wing loading than #26, for a faster glide. It is excellent for indoor and outdoor flying.

REQUIRED: one 4" × 6" index card
one 2" × 3½" business card
scissors or razor blade
tape
one plastic straw

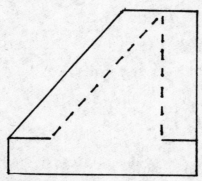

Full-Size Main Wing Pattern

Full-Size Foreplane Pattern

27a). Fold 4″ × 6″ card and 2″ × 3½″ business card in half width-wise. Using the patterns provided, trace the sketches onto folded index card (main wing) and folded business card (foreplane). Be sure to align fold with bottom of pattern. Cut according to patterns.

27b). Cut and fold leading edge slats on foreplane; cut and fold leading edge slats and rudders on main wing.

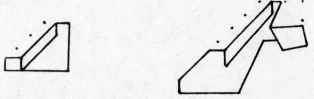

27c). Tape the foreplane on top of the straw and tape the main wing underneath the straw, as shown.

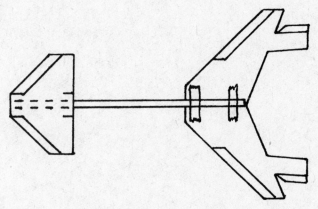

This missile was designed to fly right side up or upside down or on its side. It does not have any airfoil at all, which shows in its glide angle.

REQUIRED: four 2″ × 3½″ business cards
tape
ruler
scissors or razor blade
one plastic straw

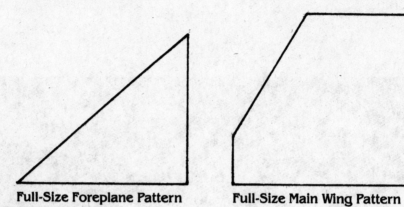

Full-Size Foreplane Pattern   Full-Size Main Wing Pattern

28a). Using the patterns provided, fold four business cards in half widthwise, and trace and cut two to match each pattern, making sure to align folds with the pattern bottoms. (Trace patterns, if you like.)

28b). Keeping the cards folded, tape folded edges together on both sides, as shown, and unfold to form an "X."

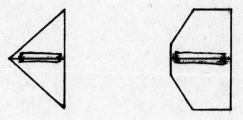

28c). Cut a ½" "+" at one end of a straw, and a ½" "X" at the other (so that the foreplane is turned 45 degrees more than the main wing). Insert "wings" (a drop of glue will fasten them very securely).

DESIGN 29

This is a high-speed "high apartment window" type of plane. It has a high wing loading and a cruciform tail for stability. The flaps add lift while keeping the airplane from going too fast. Of course, flaps are optional. If you delete the flaps, your plane will require a different trim setting than the one in the photo.

REQUIRED: one 4″ × 6″ index card
one tail section from design #28
scissors or razor blade
tape
one plastic straw
five paper clips

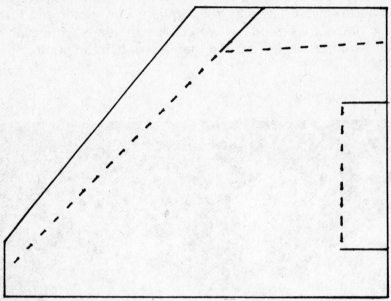

Full-Size Wing Pattern

29a). Fold 4″ × 6″ index card in half widthwise, trace, and cut according to pattern. Be sure to align fold with bottom of pattern.

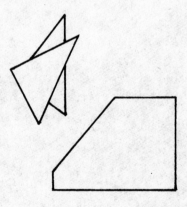

29b). Cut winglets and flaps according to sketch.

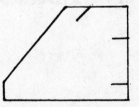

29c). Fold winglets and leading edge slats.

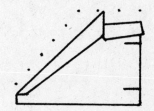

29d). Before mounting tail section from design #28, fold tail flat and cut elevators as shown. Tape wings and tail to straw, in positions shown. Attach paper clips to nose.

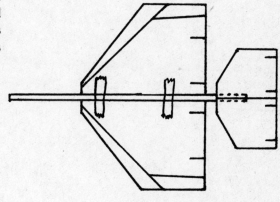

DESIGN 30

I have saved the best for last with this one. This is a canard with a forward-swept main wing. It flies surprisingly well, despite its alien appearance. It uses conventional trim tabs as well as a canard foreplane.

REQUIRED: one 4″ × 6″ index card
scissors or razor blade
tape
straw
foreplane from design #25
one or two paper clips

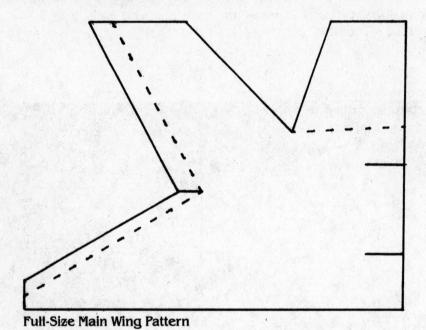

Full-Size Main Wing Pattern

30a). Fold 4″ × 6″ index card in half widthwise, trace, and cut, according to sketch. Make sure to align fold with bottom of pattern. Cut elevators.

30b). Fold rudders and leading edge slats according to sketch.

30c). Tape foreplane from design #25 on top of a straw according to sketch. Tape main wing underneath straw, as shown. Attach one or two paper clips to nose, as desired.

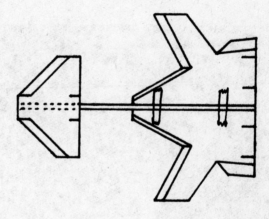

MODIFIED SLOW FLYERS

These two airplanes were modified for slow flight. Their extra lift modifications allow them to fly at far slower speeds than standard designs do. They incorporate flaps, leading edge slots, and airbrakes. These are just two of the many different combinations that can be created.

a). This is a modified #1. Notice the different type of flap cut in.

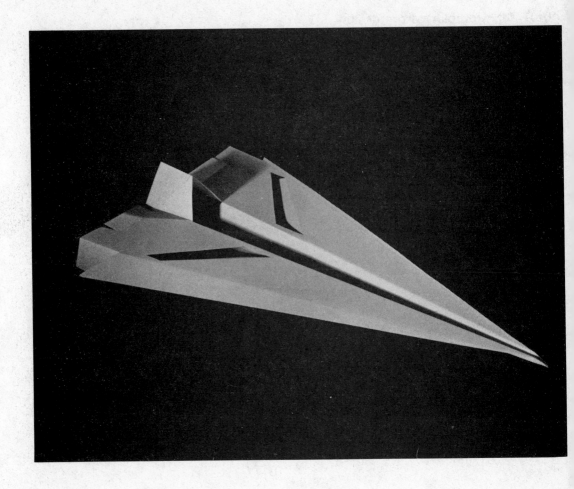

b). This is a modified #5. Leading edge slats, flaps, and airbrakes have been added.

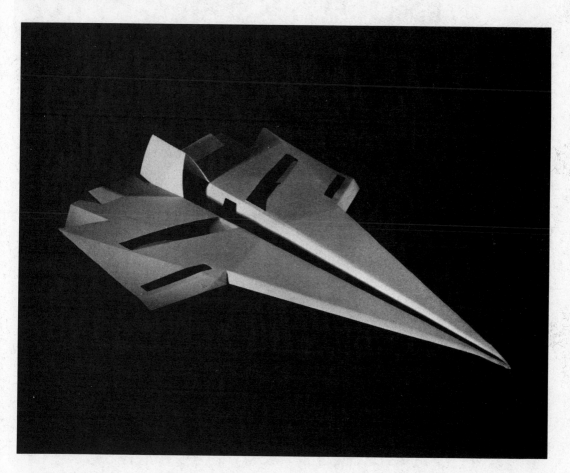

PETER VOLLHEIM works full time for a company that makes architectural scale models, but he has still found time to construct a Glasair from scratch.

He lives with his wife and son in Nashua, New Hampshire.